toys to knit

toys to knit

Tracy Chapman

COLLINS & BROWN

www.chrysalisbooks.co.uk

I dedicate this book to my mum

First published in Great Britain in 2005 by
Collins & Brown
The Chrysalis Building
Bramley Road
London W10 6SP

An imprint of **Chrysalis** Books Group plc

Copyright © Collins & Brown 2005
Text and patterns copyright © Tracy Chapman 2005

1 2 3 4 5 6 7 8 9

British Library Cataloguing-in-Publication Data:
A catalogue record for this book is available from the
British Library.

ISBN 1-84340-305-6

Designers: **Penny Stock** and **Gemma Wilson**
Project editors: **Nicola Hodgson** and **Fiona Corbridge**
Pattern checker: **Emma King**

Reproduction by **Classicscan**
Printed and bound by **SNP Leefung, China**

Contents

Introduction

Childhood is a magical time in all of our lives and should be captured and treasured. The collection that is *Toys to Knit* is a culmination of many years of research and memories.

I was very fortunate as a child, as some of my earliest recollections were of knitting! We would have day trips to my families' homes only to find my aunties rummaging excitedly through their huge stocks of yarns deciding on what to make next!

My first lessons in knitting were passed on to me by my mum who still knits to this day and who helped me enormously with this book. She patiently taught me the craft when I was a child and my earliest projects included toys and dolls clothes! From that moment I was hooked! I'd help mum sew up and stuff the various and very beautiful toys that she had made for the local fete. I'd proudly carry them in my own handmade bag.

I would spend all my free time knitting collecting yarns, needles and patterns – something I still do to this day!

Toys to Knit is a wonderful collection of my very own special memories. A basic doll that has many guises! An elephant to cuddle and nursery toys just the right size for tiny hands to hold – all play a part in that magical time of growing up.

In today's busy hi-tech world, I decided that a collection such as this would be an ideal companion to anyone with little ones in their life! And of course a must for anyone who has special memories of their own.

These pages contain much of the best of my collection, representing ideal gifts for babies and toddlers just learning about life.

This book is for children everywhere!

Happy Knitting!

Tracy Chapman

Dolls

This section of the book gives you the basic doll patterns. These basic patterns can be amended and adapted into the dolls shown later in the book such as the sailor boy and the fairy doll. Once you have mastered the simple pattern on pages 10–11, you can experiment with different facial expressions and hairstyles.

Basic doll

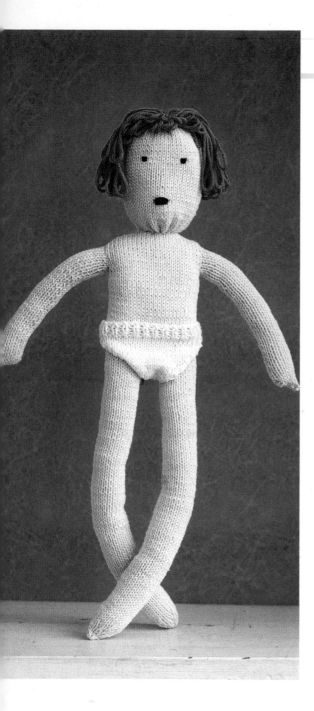

This Basic Doll pattern is the foundation for all the dolls in this book. Turn to page 13 for a selection of clothes to suit her every mood and social engagement. Then meet her friends Ballerina Belle, Artie the Sailor, Fairy Longlegs, Japanese Doll and Rag Doll.

MATERIALS

- **Rowan Cotton Glace:**
  1 x pale pink 799
  1 x light brown 730
  1 x white 726
- Black and pink embroidery thread for eyes and mouth
- Needles: 3mm/ UK size 11
- Toy stuffing

For all main body pieces, use pale pink.

HEAD
Cast on 21 sts.
1st row: K.
2nd row: K1, inc in next st, P to last stitch, inc in next st, k1 (23 sts).
3rd row: K.
4th row: As row 2 (25 sts).
5th row: K.
6th row: K1, P to last st, k1.
Continue in stocking stitch, without further shaping, for 32 rows.
Next row: K2tog twelve times, k1 (13 sts).
Next row: P.
Next row: K2tog six times, k1 (6 sts).
Cast off.
Make another piece to match.

LEGS
Cast on 24 sts.
St st 64 rows.
Decrease as follows:
Next row: K1,* k2tog, k2, rep from * to last 3 sts, k2tog, k1 (18 sts).
Next row: P.
Next row: K1, *k2tog, k2, rep from * to last 1 st, k1 (11 sts).
Next row: P.
Next row: K1, * k2tog, k2, rep from * to last 1 st, k1.
Next row: P.
Next row: K1, * k2tog, k2, rep from * to last 2 sts, k2 (9 sts).
Next row: P.
Break thread and draw through remaining 9 sts and secure. Make another leg.

BODY

Cast on 28 sts.
Stocking stitch for 36 rows.
Cast off 4 sts at the beg of next 4 rows (12 sts).
Cast off remaining 12 sts.
Make another piece the same.

ARMS

Cast on 16 sts.
Stocking stitch 50 rows.
Cast off 4 sts at beg of next 4 rows.
Make another arm.

TO MAKE UP BASIC DOLL

Sew in all ends. Join head pieces, using mattress stitch, and stuff firmly. Join the two body pieces in the same way and stuff. Join seams of legs, stuff firmly and attach to bottom of body. Fold and close seams on arms. Attach to main body. Attach head to complete the doll, ensuring that the neck is stuffed sufficiently to support the head.

HAIR

To make the hair, begin at the back of neck: sew a loop, then secure with a small stitch. Continue working in this manner until whole head is covered. Make the fringe in the same way, using shorter loops.

FEATURES

Sew features on the face as illustrated, using black embroidery thread for the eyes and pink for the lips.

KNICKERS

Use white.
Cast on 24 sts.
Work in k1 p1 rib for 4 rows.
Stocking stitch 4 rows.
Next row: Dec 1 st at each end of next and every following alt row until 10 st rem.
Next row: K2tog to end (5 sts).
Stocking stitch 3 rows.
Next row: Inc in every st (10 sts).
Next row: Inc 1 st at each end of next and every following alt row until there are 24 sts.
Stocking stitch 4 rows.
Work in k1 p1 rib for 4 rows.
Cast off.
Fold in half and join the side seams.

Clothes

Here you'll find a range of outfits that fit all the dolls that every child would love. Ideas include a pink ballerina costume, a cheeky sailor outfit, an ethereal fairy dress, Japanese geisha outfit, rag doll top and skirt, an eskimo jacket and a floppy hat.

All the clothes are interchangeable, and fit the basic doll patterns given on pages 10–11. Once you've tried these, experiment with different colours and yarns to create your own unique wardrobe of clothes and give each of your toys their own unique character.

Basic wardrobe

The Basic Doll has a set of mix and match outfits to choose from: a wrap top, a pretty skirt with a motif around the hem, a Fair Isle jumper with a snowflake pattern, and a pair of snug trousers. Knit her the whole set and she'll always look perfectly turned out – and ready for any adventure.

Wrap top

MATERIALS
- **Rowan Cotton Glace:**
  1 x purple 815
- Needles: 3mm/ UK size 11

Cast on 28 sts.
Stocking stitch 28 rows.
Next row: K9, cast off centre 10 sts and K to end.
Working on these 9 sts only, work 2 rows in stocking stitch.
Next row: K1, P to last 1 st, k1.
Next row: K1, pick up loop before next stitch and knit into back of it; knit to end (19 sts).
Continue increasing in this manner on the front edge until there are 28 sts.
Work 1 row.
Next row (RS facing): Cast on 31 sts and K to the end.
Cast off.
With wrong side of work facing, rejoin yarn to remaining sts using stocking

stitch. Work 1 row.
Next row: K1, P to last stitch, k1.
Next row: K to last stitch, pick up loop before stitch and K into the back of it, k1.
Repeat the last two rows and continue increasing in this manner, on the front edge only, until there are 28 sts.
Complete to match first side.
Cast off.

SLEEVES
Cast on 22 sts.
Work 6 rows in stocking stitch.
Next row: Increase 1 st at each end of this and following 4th row, until there are 26 sts.
Work 27 rows in stocking stitch.
Cast off.
Make another sleeve to match.

TO MAKE UP WRAP TOP
Fold sleeves in half lengthways and sew in place on top of

shoulder. Join sleeve and side seams.

STRIPED KNICKERS

MATERIALS
- **Rowan Cotton Glace**
  1 x purple 815
  1 x white 726

This version is worked in stripes, beginning with the purple. Change colour on every third row. Follow instructions for Knickers on page 11.

Skirt

MATERIALS
- **Rowan Cotton Glace:**
  1 x lilac 811 (A)
  1 x white 726 (B)
- Needles: 3.25mm/ UK size10
- Crochet hook: 3.25mm
- Small button

Using main yarn, cast on 140 sts.

Garter stitch (every row knit) for 4 rows.
Stocking stitch 2 rows.
Next row: Using the Fair Isle technique, set motif as illustrated in chart, using contrast yarn.
Continue in stocking stitch for a further 24 rows.
Decrease row.
Next row: K2, * k2tog, repeat from * to last 2 sts, k2 (68 sts).
Next row: P.
Next row: K4, * k2tog, k1,

repeat from * to last 4 sts, k4 (48 sts).
Stocking stitch 2 rows.
Cast off.

TO MAKE UP SKIRT
Darn in all ends on the skirt and join sides by mattress stitch. Leave approx. 4cm open at the top. Sew on a small button and crochet a chain to use as a loop.

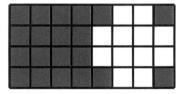

■ A
□ B

Fair Isle jumper

MATERIALS
- **Rowan All Seasons Cotton:**
  1 x cream 178 (A)
  1 x light blue 192 (B)
- Needles: 4.5mm/ UK size 7

FRONT
Cast on 25 sts.
Work k1 p1 rib for 4 rows.

Continue in stocking stitch for 4 rows.
Next row: Set snowflake motif as follows, using Fair Isle technique. K6, next 13 sts follow chart, k6. Work 13-row chart to complete motif. Continue in main shade only, working a further 4 rows in stocking stitch.
Work 4 rows in k1 p1 rib.
Cast off.

BACK
Work as front, omitting the motif.

SLEEVES
Cast on 22 sts.
Work 6 rows in stocking stitch.
Next row: Decrease 1 st at each end of this and every following 4th row until there are 14 sts.
Work 1 row without shaping.
Next row: Work 4 rows of k1 p1 rib.
Cast off.
Make another sleeve to match

TO MAKE UP THE FAIR ISLE JUMPER
As for Teddy Bear's Blue Sweater (see page 53).

Trousers

MATERIALS

- **Rowan All Seasons Cotton:**
  1 x light blue 192
- Needles: 4.5mm/ UK size 7
- Elastic: 20cm

Cast on 25 sts.
Knit 2 rows.
Next row: Beginning with a knit row, work in stocking stitch for 50 rows.

Next row: Work 4 rows in k1 p1 rib. Cast off.
Make another piece to match.

TO MAKE UP TROUSERS

Darn in all loose ends. Starting at bottom of leg, join seams using mattress stitch. Work until 4cm from rib. Join both legs at centre seam. Sew elastic around top of trousers to form a waistband.

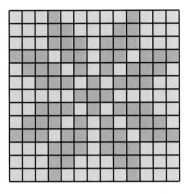

☐ A

☐ B

Ballerina clothes

This graceful ballerina has all the right accessories to use in her exciting performances – a tutu, ballet shoes, leg warmers and even a delicate necklace!

MATERIALS
- **Rowan Cotton Glace:**
  1 x pale pink 799
  1 x brown 816
  1 x dark pink 724
  1 x white 726
- White DK oddments for leg warmers
- Black and pink embroidery thread for eyes and mouth
- Needles: 3mm/ UK size 11
- Crochet hook: 3mm
- Ballet net: 25cm in either light pink or white
- Bias binding to match net
- Press studs
- 2 sequins, 2 beads, embroidery cotton
- Toy stuffing

DOLL
As Basic Doll. Use pale pink.

HAIR
As Basic Doll. Use brown.

KNICKERS
As for Basic Doll. Use white.

WRAP TOP
As for Wrap Top, on page 14.

Use dark pink.

TUTU
Fold the ballet net in half lengthways and gently gather it to fit around the waist of the doll. Tack as you go, then sew securely. Take the bias binding and fold it over the gathered waist edge of the net. Pin and sew in place, covering the tacking stitches. To finish, sew the press stud parts to either end of the waistband. Trim the tutu to the desired length.

SHOES
Use dark pink.
Using the crochet hook, make a foundation ring of 8 ch, join with a slip stitch and work in rounds.
Round 1: Make 2 ch; work 8tr into ring, working over loose end.
Round 2: As round 1.
Round 3: As round 1.
Continue working in this way until shoe fits securely on the foot.
To finish, crochet two chains on either side of shoe to use as straps.
Make another shoe to match.

NECKLACE
Thread two sequins, in different colours and shapes, on to a piece of embroidery cotton. Thread on a bead, then thread the cotton back through the two sequins.

LEG WARMERS
Use white DK oddments.
Cast on 24 sts.
Continue in k2 p2 rib for 40 rows.
Cast off in pattern.
Make another leg warmer to match.
To finish: join side seams using mattress stitch.

HAIRBAND
Use dark pink.
The hairband is made by casting on 5 sts, and working in stocking stitch until when the hairband is slighty stretched, it fits across the top of the head.

Sailor clothes

Watching the ships in a busy harbour inspired me to design this cheeky chap, full of tall tales about his journeys around the world and encounters with monsters of the deep.

MATERIALS
- **Rowan Cotton Glace:**
  1 x pale pink 799
  1 x brown 816
- **Rowan Handknit Cotton:**
  1 x navy 277
  1 x white 263
- Black and pink embroidery thread for eyes and mouth
- Needles: 3mm/ UK size 11
- Elastic: 20cm
- Toy stuffing

DOLL
As Basic Doll. Use pale pink.

TUNIC TOP
Use navy.

BACK
Cast on 28 sts.
Stocking stitch until 14cm long.
Cast off.

FRONT
Cast on 28 sts.
Stocking stitch 26 rows.
Divide for neck: k14, work on these stitches only.

Next row: P.
Decrease 1 st on neck edge on this and following 7 alternate rows (6 sts).
Stocking stitch 3 rows.
Cast off.
Rejoin yarn to remaining 14 sts and reverse shaping to match first side.

TUNIC INSET
Use navy and white.
Using white, cast on 20 sts.
Work in stocking stitch throughout.
Work 11 rows.
Change to navy and K 1 row.
Cast off.

SLEEVES
Use navy.
Cast on 22 sts.
Work 6 rows in stocking stitch.
Next row: Increase 1 st at each end of this and every following 4th row, until there are 26 sts.
Stocking stitch 20 rows.
Cast off.
Make a second sleeve.

TROUSERS
Use navy.
Cast on 35 sts.
Work 2 rows in garter stitch (every row knit).
Stocking stitch 74 rows.
Next row: K4, * yfwd k2tog, repeat from * four times, K to end of row.
P 2 rows.
Cast off.
Make another piece the same.

COLLAR
Use navy and white.
Using navy, cast on 48 sts.
Work 4 rows in garter stitch.
Change to white yarn.
Next row: K2tog tbl, k12, k2tog tbl, k16, k2tog, k12, k2tog (44 sts).
Row 6: K2tog, K to the last 2 sts, k2tog (42 sts).
Row 7: Rejoin navy, k2tog tbl, k10, k2tog tbl, k14, k2tog, k10, k2tog (38 sts).
Row 8: As row 6 (36 sts).
Row 9: Rejoin white, k2tog tbl, k8, k2tog tbl, k12, k2tog, k8, k2tog (32 sts).

Row 10: As row 6 (30 sts). Break off white yarn and continue in navy throughout.
Row 11: K2tog tbl, k6, k2tog tbl, k10, k2tog, k6, k2tog (26 sts).
Row 12: K2tog, P to last 2 sts, k2tog (24 sts).
Row 13: K2tog tbl, k4, k2tog tbl, k8, k2tog, k4, k2tog (20 sts).
Row 14: As row 12 (18 sts).
Row 15: K2tog tbl, k2, k2tog tbl, k6, k2tog, k2, k2tog (14 sts).
Row 16: As row 12 (12 sts). Cast off.

HAT
Use navy.
Cast on 32 sts.
Work 3 rows in garter stitch.
Row 4: Change to white. Sl1, P to the last st, k1.
Work 2 rows in garter stitch.
Row 7: Sl1, k2, * increase once in the next st, k4, repeat from * to the last 4 sts. Increase once in the next st, k3 (38 sts).
Row 8 (and every following alternate row): Sl1, P to the last st, k1.
Row 9: Sl1, k2, * increase once in the next st, k5, repeat from * to the last 5 sts. Increase once in the next st, k4 (44 sts).
Row 11: Sl1, (k5, k2tog) six

times, k1 (38 sts).
Row 13: Sl1, K to the end of the row.
Row 15: Sl1, (k4, k2tog) six times, k1 (32 sts).
Row 17: Sl1, (k3, k2tog) six times, k1 (26 sts).
Row 19: Sl1, (k2, k2tog) six times, k1 (20 sts).
Row 21: Sl1, (k1, k2tog) six times, k1 (14 sts).
Row 23: Sl1, (k2tog) six times, k1 (8 sts).
Break off yarn and draw through remaining stitches and fasten off.

TO MAKE UP SAILOR
Darn in all ends. Join seam on hat and stitch open side. Join shoulders on tunic, sew inset into position as illustrated, attach sleeves and sew side and sleeve seams using mattress stitch. Make a twisted cord and thread through eyelets. Starting at bottom of leg, join trouser seams using mattress stitch. Work until 4cm from rib. Join both legs at centre seam. Thread needle with elastic and sew a length around top of trousers to form a waistband.

Fairy clothes

Share magical times with this enchanting fairy. She has very long legs, delicate wings and a beautiful organza skirt that looks like gossamer.

MATERIALS

- **Rowan Cotton Glace:**
  1 x pale pink 799
  1 x white 726
- **Rowan All Seasons Cotton:**
  1 x gold 205
- Black and pink embroidery thread for eyes and mouth
- Needles: 3mm/ UK size 11; 3.25m/ UK size 10
- Crochet hook: 3.25mm
- White organza: 50cm
- Bias binding tape: 30cm
- Narrow silver ribbon: 1m
- Pins, needle and thread
- Press stud
- 2 buttons
- Toy stuffing

DOLL
As Basic Doll*. Use pale pink.

*LEGS
Stocking stitch 84 rows (not 64 rows).

HAIR
As Basic Doll. Use gold, doubled.

KNICKERS
As Basic Doll. Use white.

TOP
As Sailor Top, front sections. Use white and 3.25mm/ UK size 10 needles.

The top is constructed by joining the front sections on one side, using mattress stitch. This will be the back seam. Fold the outside edges into the middle and catch the shoulders together to form a jacket. Sew on the buttons, and crochet two small button loops.

WINGS
Use white and 3mm/ UK size 11 needles.
Cast on 42 sts.
Working in garter stitch throughout (every row knit), work 36 rows.
Eyelet row: K2, * yfwd, k2tog, repeat from * to last 2 sts, k2.

This forms the holes for the ribbon to be threaded through.
Continue in garter stitch for a further 18 rows.
Cast off.

Thread ribbon through the eyelet holes, pull to gather slightly and tie ribbon around doll's waist to form wings.

SKIRT
Fold the white organza along the width, forming a long rectangle, and tack along the top using running stitch. Gather the fabric to fit around the waist of the fairy and sew securely. Sandwich the raw edge of the organza in between the bias binding tape and pin, tack and sew in place. Attach the press stud. Trim off any loose threads. Wrap small sections of ribbon around the ankles and sew in place.

Japanese clothes

This pretty girl from the Far East wears a brightly coloured traditional kimono and has an upswept hairstyle, decorated with blossoms. Her calm, meditative air makes her a good friend to have around, and she's the perfect confidante. She'll be a welcome guest in anyone's home.

MATERIALS
- **Rowan Cotton Glace:**
  1 x pale pink 799
  1 x white 746
  2 x red 741
- **Rowan Yorkshire Tweed DK:**
  1 x grey 354
- **Rowan 4-ply Soft:**
  1 x light blue 373
- Black and pink embroidery thread for eyes and mouth
- Needles: 3mm/ UK size 11
- Ribbon: 50cm, light blue
- Roses: 3 x mini ribbon roses
- Toy stuffing

DOLL
As Basic Doll. Use pale pink.

HAIR
As Basic Doll. Use grey.
Follow instructions for long hair sections on Rag Doll, using the same technique, but only around the outer hairline. When completed, gather up at crown of head and secure with same yarn. Allow the loose ends to fall equally around the tied hair and gather up to form a bun. Sew securely and attach a rose on the side of the head at the front.

KIMONO
Use red.

BACK
Cast on 34 sts.
K 2 rows.
Next row: K.
Next row: K2, P to last 2 sts, k2.
Repeat the last two rows until work measures 15cm.
Continue in stocking stitch, knitting the first two and last two stitches of every row *
until work measures 27cm from cast-on.

SHAPE SHOULDERS
Cast off 6 sts at beginning of next 4 rows (10 sts).
Cast off remaining 10 sts.

FRONT
Work as back until * (22cm).
Divide for front.
K17, turn work, k1, P to last st, k1.
Continue on these 17 sts only, until work measures 27cm from cast-on.
Cast off 6 sts (11 sts).
Work 1 row.
Cast off 6 sts (5 sts).
Cast off remaining 5 sts.
Rejoin yarn to remaining 17 sts and work to match first side.

SLEEVES
Cast on 44 sts.
Work 6 rows in garter stitch.
Continue in stocking stitch until work measures 9cm.
Cast off.
Make another sleeve to match.

TO MAKE UP KIMONO
Darn in all loose ends. Join shoulder seams using mattress stitch. Attach sleeves and join

sleeve and side seams. Press
work to keep open side seams
flat.

KNICKERS
As Basic Doll. Use white.

BACK PILLOW
Use light blue.
Cast on 25 sts.
Work 25 rows in stocking
stitch.
Next row (RS): P 1 row – to
make fold.
Next row (WS): Continue in
stocking stitch, starting with a
purl row, and work 24 rows.
Cast off.

TO MAKE UP THE BACK
PILLOW
Darn in all loose ends. Fold in
half and sew sides using
mattress stitch. Stuff slightly
and close last side. Attach
ribbon to pad as illustrated.

Rag doll clothes

With her distinctive golden plaits and bubbly fringe, Rag Doll cuts a tall, striking figure. She's happy to sit dangling her long legs over a shelf, watching everything that's going on. She's all ready for summer days in a cute sleeveless top and skirt with interesting hem detail, embellished with an embroidered daisy.

MATERIALS
- **Rowan Cotton Glace:**
  1 x pale pink 799
  1 x white 726
- **Rowan All Seasons Cotton:**
  1 x yellow 205
  1 x pink 202
  1 x lilac 181
- Black and pink embroidery thread for eyes and mouth
- Needles: 3mm/ UK size 11, 4.5mm/ UK size 7
- Crochet hook: 3.25mm/ UK size ??
- Beads
- Toy stuffing

DOLL
As Basic Doll. Use pale pink and 3mm needles.
Legs: work an additional 20 rows for extra length.

HAIR
As Basic Doll. Use yellow.
To make fringe, follow instructions for Basic Doll.

To make the longer sections of hair, cut lengths of yarn measuring 60cm and fold in half. Using a crochet hook and

starting at the back of the fringe, insert hook and draw through folded end of yarn; secure by threading long ends

through. Tighten up. Repeat
this technique in rows across
the head, working down
towards the neck.
To make plaits, divide the hair
into two halves and secure
gently. Tidy up both sections
and divide each of them into
three equal bunches. Plait
down the length. Tie with yarn
in a bow.

FEATURES

Using black and pink
embroidery thread, darn face
as illustrated.

KNICKERS

As Basic Doll. Use white.

SKIRT

Use pink and 4.5mm needles.
Cast on 74 sts.
K 1 row.
Commence pattern:
1st row: K.
2nd row: P.
3rd row: K1, * (k2tog) three
times, (yfwd, k1) six times,
repeat from * to last st, k1.
4th row: K.
Repeat these 4 rows once more.

With WS facing, work a further 28 rows without shaping.
Next row: K2tog to end of row (37 sts).
Work a further 6 rows in garter stitch.
Cast off.

TO MAKE UP THE SKIRT
Darn in all loose ends and embroider a 'lazy daisy' motif on bottom of skirt above the pattern sequence.

SLEEVELESS TOP
Use lilac and 4.5mm needles.

BACK
Using lilac, cast on 25 sts.
Work 4 rows in moss stitch.
Work a further 32 rows in stocking stitch.
Cast off.

FRONT
Using lilac, cast on 25 sts.
Work 4 rows in moss stitch.
Work a further 14 rows in stocking stitch.
Next row: Divide for front.
K13, turn work and P to end.
Next row: K to last 2 sts, k2,

turn work and P to end.
Work a further 2 rows without shaping.
Next row: Decrease 1 st at neck edge.
Repeat the last 3 rows until 8 sts remain.
Cast off.

Rejoin yarn to remaining 12 sts and complete to match first side.

TO MAKE UP THE TOP
Darn in all loose ends. Join all seams using mattress stitch. Join shoulder and side seams.

Eskimo Jacket

Make this beautiful eskimo jacket which fits the basic doll pattern, to go with a pair of the trousers (shown on page 17) or a skirt (shown on pages 14–15).

MATERIALS
- 1 x **Rowan All Seasons Cotton 191 Jersey**
- 1 x **Rowan All Seasons Cotton 178 Organic**
- 4.50mm Needles

ML – On the right side of the work knit to the position of the loop. Knit the next stitch, but do not allow the loop to drop off the left hand needle. Bring the yarn to the front between the two needles and wind the yarn around your left thumb.

Take the yarn to the back again between the needles and knit into the same stitch remaining on the left hand needle – so making two stitches out of the original one. Slip the stitch off the left hand needle.

Place both stitches back on the left hand needle and knit them together through the back of the loops to complete the stitch.

MAIN BODY & SLEEVES
(worked in one piece)

Starting at lower edge of back and using 191 Jersey cast on 26 stitches
Work 16 rows in stocking stitch.

SLEEVE SHAPING
With RS facing and working in st st throughout cast on 3 sts at the beg of the next 8 rows (50)sts
Work 8 rows without further shaping

NECK SHAPING
Knit 21, cast off centre 8sts, knit to end.
Working on first set of 21 sts only and beg with a purl row stocking stitch 7 rows.
Next row RS (neck edge) Cast on 4 sts knit to end (25)sts
Next row WS Cast off 3 sts at sleeve edge on next and three following alt rows (13)sts
Next row RS beginning with a knit row, work 16 rows in stocking stitch
Cast off
With WS facing rejoin yarn to remaining 21sts
Beginning with a purl row work 6 rows in stocking stitch
Next row WS (neck edge) cast on 4sts purl to end.
Next row RS cast off 3 sts at sleeve edge on the next and three following alt rows (13)sts
Next row WS beginning with a purl row, work 16 rows in stocking stitch
Cast off

HOOD
Using 178 organic cast on 43 stitches
1st row K1, * ML k1 rep from * to end
2nd row purl
3rd row as 1st
4th row change to 191 jersey and purl
Next row RS beginning with a knit row, continue in stocking stitch until work measures 6cm from cast on.
Cast off

MAKING UP

Darn in all loose ends. Fold hood in half with loops at the front, join back seam (cast off edge) together by using mattress stitch. Attach to main body of jacket easing the side edges around neck shaping. Starting a cuff join sleeve seams in the same manner leaving a 3cm vent at the bottom of the side edges.

Make two twisted cords each measuring 15cm and attach to jacket at the bottom of the hood on the neck edge.

Floppy brimmed hat

This georgeous floppy hat is perfect for a lazy day in the sunshine. It can be knitted in any colour to go with the outfit you make for any of the dolls in the book. Here it is modelled by the ballerina doll, but it could work equally well on the rag doll or the basic dolly on page 14.

MATERIALS
1 x 50g ball of the following
- **Rowan All Seasons Cotton 178 Ecru**
- 4.50mm needles

CROWN
Cast on 40 stitches
Work six rows in stocking stitch.

Shape crown
7th row * (k6, K2tog) rep from * to end (35)sts
8th row Purl
9th row * (K5, K2tog) rep from * to end (30)sts
10th row Purl
11th row * (K4, K2tog) rep from * to end (25)sts
12th row Purl
13th row * (K3, K2tog) rep from * to end (20)sts
14th row purl
15th row * (K2, K2tog) rep from * to end (15)sts
16th row purl
17th row * (K1, K2tog) rep from * to end (10)sts
18th row purl
Break yarn and draw through remaining 10 stitches and secure.

BRIM
With RS facing pick up and knit 40stitches along cast on edge of crown.

2nd row WS Inc in every stitch (80)sts
3rd row RS * K3, inc 1 rep from * to end (100)sts
4th row purl
5th row knit
6th row purl
7th row * K4, inc 1 rep from * to end (120)sts
8th row purl
9th row knit
10th row purl
11th row (eyelet row) K2 * yfwd K2tog rep from * to end
12th row purl
13th row knit
14th row purl
cast off

MAKING UP
Darn in all loose ends.
To complete frilly edge fold along eyelet row and slip stitch into place.
Join seam by using mattress stitch.

Boys button-up shoes

MATERIALS

- 1 x Ball **Rowan Cotton Glace** 746 Nightshade
- 4 small buttons
- 3mm needles

Cast on 28 stitches
Work four rows in single rib
*k1, p1 rep from * to end.
Next RS work a further six
rows in garter stitch every row
knit.
Decrease as follows:
11th row k3 *k2tog k2 rep
from * to last st, k1 (22) sts
12th row knit
13th row k2 *k2tog k2 rep
from * to end (17)sts
14th row knit
15th row k1 *k2tog k2 rep
from * to end (13)sts
16th row knit
17th row k1 *k2tog rep from *
to end (7) sts
Break yarn draw through
tightly and secure.
Make another to match.

MAKING UP

Darn all loose ends. Join rib by
back stitching and main panel
by picking up stitches from
either side and secure. With
seam at the back sew two
buttons on to the front of
each shoe as illustrated.

Girls lace-up shoes

MATERIALS

- 1 x ball **Rowan cotton glace** 747 Candy-floss
- Oddments of Rowan 4 ply Soft 373 Splash
- 3mm needles
- 3.25 mm crochet hook

Cast on 28 stitches
Work two rows in garter stitch.
Every row knit.
Next row (eyelets) k1, *yfwd
k2tog rep from * to last stitch,
k1
Next row WS knit
Next row RD beginning with a
knit row, work six rows in
stocking stitch.
Decrease as follows
11th row (RS) k3, *k2 tog k2
rep from * to last stitch, k1 (22)
sts
12th row purl
13th row k2, *k2tog k2 rep
from * to end (17)sts
14th row purl
15th row k1, *k2tog k2 rep
from * to end (13) sts
16th row purl
17th row k1, *k2tog rep from *
to end (7) sts
Break yarn draw through
tightly and secure
Make another to match

TIES

Using crochet hook and
oddment of yarn, chaing 22cm
fasten off.
Make another to match.

MAKING UP

Darn in all loose ends. Join
seams by using mattress stitch.
With seam at the back, begin
in the centre front and thread
the ties through the row of
eyelets. Tie in a bow.

Animals

Each of the animals in this section is ideal to knit for a child or adult and all would make great gifts. Take a look at the cheeky monkey or the solemn penguin. Each has its own character and style and will become an individual each time you make them. The only problem will be in deciding who to make first. Mousie Mousie is so cute who could resist! Robbie the fish and Mr Bumble would be loved by a baby or toddler, while Rabbit and Kangaroo would suit an older child or adult. Reggie the Snake would make anyone laugh and Teddy Bear and Loulou the Elephant are great for hugs. The choice is yours.

Tucker the monkey

This appealing little monkey, with a heart-shaped face, is full of charm. He's curious about life and dressed for adventure in a snazzy waistcoat and scarf. Tucker is full of mischief and great fun to have around.

MATERIALS
- **Rowan Yorkshire Tweed 4-ply:**
  4 x brown 273*
  1 x fawn 264
  1 x red 274
- **Rowan Summer Tweed:**
  1 x green 527
- Black embroidery thread for eyes, nose and mouth
- Needles: 3mm/ UK size 11
- Double-pointed needles: 2 x 3mm/ UK size 11
- Toy stuffing

* Yarn to be used doubled (apart from ears)

BODY – BACK
Use brown.
Using the yarn doubled, cast on 12 sts.
Work 2 rows in stocking stitch.
Next row: Increase 1 st at each end of this and every following 4th row until there are 20 sts.
Work 26 rows without shaping.

SHAPE TOP OF BODY BACK
Decrease 1 st at each end of next and every following alt row until there are 6 sts.
Work 1 row.
Cast off.

BODY – FRONT (2 PIECES)
Use brown.

SIDE 1
Using the yarn doubled, cast on 6 sts.
Work 2 rows in stocking stitch.
Next row: Increase 1 st at each end of this and every following 4th row until there are 12 sts.
Work 26 rows without further shaping **.
Next row: With RS facing, decrease 1 st at END of next row and at the END of every following 4th row until there are 8 sts.
Work 1 row.
Next row: Decrease 1 st at each end of this and every following alt row until 2 sts remain.

Cast off.

SIDE 2
Work as side 1 until **.
Decrease at BEGINNING of next row and at the BEGINNING of every following 4th row until there are 8 sts.
Work 1 row.
Next row: Decrease 1 st at each end of this and every following alt row until there are 2 sts.
Cast off.

LEGS
Use brown.
Using the yarn doubled, cast on 20 sts.
Work in stocking stitch, continuing until work measures 20cm (approx. 70 rows).
Cast off.
Make another leg to match.

ARMS
Use brown.
Using the yarn doubled, cast on 16 sts.

Work in stocking stitch, continuing until work measures 16cm (approx. 56 rows).

SHAPE TOP OF ARM

K1, k2tog, k4, k2tog, k4, k2tog, k1 (13 sts).
Purl.
K1, k2tog, k7, k2tog, k1 (11 sts).
Purl.
K1, k2tog, k1, k3tog, k1, k2tog, k1 (7 sts).
Purl.
K1, k2tog, k1, k2tog, k1 (5 sts).
Purl.
Cast off.
Make another arm to match.

HEAD

Use brown.
Using the yarn doubled, cast on 9 sts.
Work 2 rows in stocking stitch.
Next row: Increase 1 st at each end of this and every following alt row until there are 21 sts.
Work a further 20 rows without shaping.
Next row: Decrease 1 st at each end of this and every following row until there are 9 sts.
Cast off.
Make another piece to match.

TAIL

Use brown, using the yarn doubled.
Follow pattern for Mousie Mousie – Tail (see page 00).
Work until it measures 35cm.

HANDS AND FEET – 2 PIECES FOR EACH

Use fawn.
Cast on 20 sts and work in garter stitch (every row knit) for 20 rows.
Break yarn and draw through stitches.
Fasten off.

FACE

Use fawn.
Cast on 8 sts and work in stocking stitch.
K 1 row.
Next row: K1, P to last st, k1.
Next row: Increase 1 st at each

end of this and every following row until there are 20 sts, then on following 4th row to make 22 sts.

Work 9 rows without further shaping.

Decrease 1 st at each end of next and 2 following alt rows (16 sts).

Work 1 row.

Next row: K8, turn work, k1, P to the last st, k1.

Working on these stitches only, decrease 1 st at each end of next and every following alt row (4 sts).

K1, P to last st, k1.

Next row: K.

Next row: P.

K2tog twice (2 sts).

Break yarn and draw through. Fasten off.

Rejoin yarn to remaining 8 sts and complete to match first side.

EARS

Use brown.

Using yarn single, cast on 10 sts and work in garter stitch.

K 4 rows.

Next row: K2tog, k6, k2tog (8 sts).

Work 3 rows without shaping.

Next row: K2tog, k4, k2tog (6 sts).

Next row: K2tog, k2, k2tog (4 sts).

Next row: K2tog twice (2 sts).

Break yarn and draw through. Fasten off.

Make another ear to match.

WAISTCOAT

Use green.

Cast on 30 sts.

Work in garter stitch.

K 1 row.

Next row: Increase 1 st at each end of row (32 sts).

Work 8 rows without shaping.

Shape armholes:

K7, cast off 2 sts, k10, cast off 2 sts, working on these 7 sts only.

K 9 rows.

Next row: Cast off 1 st, work to end.

K 1 row.

Next row: Cast off 1 st, work to end.

Work 3 rows.

Cast off.

Rejoin yarn to central 10 sts.

Work 14 rows in garter stitch.

Cast off.

Rejoin yarn to remaining 7 sts, reverse shaping to match first side.

SCARF

Use red.

Using yarn doubled, cast on 6 sts.

Work in garter stitch until scarf measures approx 25cm.

Cast off.

TO MAKE UP MONKEY

Darn in all loose ends. Join centre seams of body fronts and attach to back with mattress stitch. Stuff firmly. Sew head pieces together and graft on face. Sew arm and leg seams using mattress stitch and attach hands and feet. Using illustration as a guide, attach all body pieces. Sew on tail. Sew shoulders together on waistcoat and tie scarf loosely around neck. Embroider facial features.

Robbie the fish

Robbie's brightly coloured scales make him one of the best-looking fish in the sea. He is just the right size to tuck under your arm on a day out exploring dry land!

MATERIALS

- **Rowan Handknit Cotton:**
  2 x white 263
  1 x light blue 204
  1 x mid-blue 239
  1 x lilac 305
- **Rowan Cotton Glace:**
  1 x gold 802 (used doubled)
- Black embroidery thread for eyes
- Needles: 4mm/ UK size 8
- Toy stuffing

MAIN BODY

Use white.

Cast on 8 sts and K 1 row.

Beginning with a purl row, work in stocking stitch throughout.

Cast on 3 sts at the beginning of next two rows (14 sts).

Cast on 2 sts at the beginning of the next 4 rows (22 sts).

Work 1 row.

Next row: Increase 1 st at each end of this, and every following alt row, until there are 26 sts.

Next row: P.

Next row: Increase 1 st at each end of this and following 4 alternate rows, until there are 30 sts.

Work a further 7 rows without shaping.

Next row: Decrease 1 st at each end of this and following 4th row (26 sts).

Work 1 row.

Next row: Decrease 1 st at each end of this and every following alternate row, until there are 22 sts.

Work 1 row.

Cast off 2 sts at the beginning of the next 4 rows (14 sts).

Cast off 3 sts at the beginning of the next 2 rows (8 sts).

Cast off remaining 8 sts.

Make another piece to match.

SCALES

24 scales are used on the fish (12 on each side), and they are knitted in light blue , mid-blue and lilac.

Using the appropriate yarn, cast on 3 sts and K 2 rows.
Next row: Increase 1 st at each end of row (5 sts).
Next row: P.
Repeat the last 2 rows until there are 13 sts.
Cast off.

FIN AND TAIL

The pieces are worked in exactly the same manner as the scales. Use gold.
Using yarn doubled, cast on 8 sts and, working in k1 p1 rib, complete 1 row.
Next row: Increase 1 st at each end of this row (10 sts).
Continue increasing as before, on every row, until there are 20 sts.
Cast off.

TO MAKE UP THE FISH

Darn in all loose ends. Attach 12 of the fins to each side panel as illustrated. When joining the side panels, insert the fin along the top edge and the tail at the back. Stuff firmly. Use black embroidery thread for the eyes, and sew on lips made from a scrap of gold yarn.

Mr Bumble

Mr Bumble is a jolly little bee. He is simple to knit and enjoys buzzing around the garden.

MATERIALS
- **Rowan Handknit Cotton:**
  1 x black 252
- **Rowan Cotton Glace:**
  1 x gold 802*
- White and pink embroidery thread for eyes and mouth
- Needles: 4mm/ UK size 8
- Toy stuffing

* Yarn to be used doubled

BODY

TOP PANEL
Worked in black and gold, in stocking stitch 4 x 4 row stripes.
Using black, cast on 6 sts and work 2 rows in stocking stitch.
Increase in every stitch (12 sts).
Next row: P.
Increase in every stitch (24 sts).
Beginning with a purl row, work 29 rows in stocking stitch.
Decrease top.
Next row: K1, k2 tog, k8, k2tog, k8, k2tog, k1 (21 sts).

Beginning with a purl row, work 7 rows in stocking stitch.
Next row: K1, sl1, k1, psso, k15, k2tog, k1 (19 sts).
Next row: P.
Next row: K1, sl1, k1, psso, k13, k2tog, k1 (17 sts).
Next row: P.
Next row: K1, sl1, k1, psso, k11, k2tog, k1 (15 sts).
Next row: P.
Next row: K1, sl1, k1, psso, k9, k2tog, k1 (13 sts).
Next row: P.
Next row: Cast off 2 sts at the beginning of the next 4 rows (5 sts).
Cast off remainder.

BOTTOM PANEL
Work as for top panel, using black yarn only.

HEAD
Use black.
Cast on 6 sts.
Stocking stitch 2 rows.
Next row: Increase 1 st at each end of row (8 sts).
Stocking stitch 10 rows.
Next row: Decrease 1 st at each end of this row (6 sts).
Cast off.
Make another piece the same.

LARGE WINGS
Use black.
Cast on 12 sts.
K 2 rows.
Row 3: Increase 1 st at each end of the row (14 sts).
Repeat these 3 rows until there are 22 sts.
Next row: K2tog to end (11 sts).
Cast off.
Make another wing.

SMALL WINGS
Use black.
Cast on 8 sts.
K 2 rows.
Row 3: Increase 1 st at each end of row (10 sts).
Repeat these 3 rows until there are 18 sts.
Next row: K2tog to end (9 sts).
Cast off.
Make another wing.

TO MAKE UP THE BEE
Darn in all ends. Sew body pieces together with mattress stitch; stuff. Join head sections; attach to body. Use chain stitch to make antennae and knot the ends to form balls. Attach to head. Join wings to body. Embroider eyes and mouth.

Teddy bear

Create this enduring Teddy Bear to be someone's special friend. He will reward his owner with lots of love and loyalty. There are two different sweaters to make for him, so you can change his outfits and keep him looking stylish. He would also make a special gift for an adult bear fan.

MATERIALS
- Rowan Yorkshire Tweed DK: 4 x brown fleck 353
- Black embroidery thread for eyes and mouth
- Needles: 4mm/ UK size 8
- Toy stuffing

HEAD
Cast on 6 sts.
Work in garter stitch throughout.
Work 1 row.
Next row: Increase in every stitch (12 sts).
Work 1 row.
Next row: K1, increase into each of the next 10 sts, k1 (22 sts).
Work 1 row.

SHAPE NOSE
Next row: K1, inc 1, k7, inc 1, k6, inc 1, k7, inc 1, k1 (26 sts).
Next and every alt row: Work without shaping.
Next row: K1, inc 1, k9, inc 1, k6, inc 1, k9, inc 1, k1 (30 sts).
Next row: K1, inc 1, k11, inc 1, k6, inc 1, k11, inc 1, k1 (34 sts).
Next row: K1, inc 1, k13, inc 1, k6, inc 1, k13, inc 1, k1 (38 sts).
Next row: K1, inc 1, k15, inc 1, k6, inc 1, k15, inc 1, k1 (42 sts).
Work 2 rows without shaping.
Next row: (K1, k2tog) six times, k6, (k2tog, k1) six times (30 sts).

SHAPE HEAD
Next row: K11, inc 1, k1, inc 1, k6, inc 1, k1, inc 1, k11 (34 sts).
Next and every alt row: Work without shaping.
Next row: K12, inc 1, k1, inc 1, k8, inc 1, k1, inc 1, k12 (38 sts).
Next row: K13, inc 1, k1, inc 1, k10, inc 1, k1, inc 1, k13 (42 sts).
Next row: K14, inc 1, k1, inc 1, k12, inc 1, k1, inc 1, k14 (46 sts).
Next row: K15, inc 1, k1, inc 1, k14, inc 1, k1, inc 1, k15 (50 sts).
Next row: K16, inc 1, k1, inc 1, k16, inc 1, k1, inc 1, k16 (54 sts).
Next row: K6 (inc 1, k1) thirteen times, k16, (k1, inc 1) thirteen times, k6 (80 sts).
Work a further 13 rows without shaping.

SHAPE BACK
Next row: (K8, k2tog) to end (72 sts).
Next and every alt row: Work without shaping.
Next row: (K7, k2tog) to end (64 sts).
Next row: (K6, k2tog) to end (56 sts).
Next row (K5, k2tog) to end (48 sts).
Next row: (K4, k2tog) to end (40 sts).
Next row: (K3, k2tog) to end (32 sts).
Next row: (K2, k2tog) to end (24 sts).
Next row: (K1, k2tog) to end

(16 sts).

Next row: (K2tog) to end
(8 sts).

Cast off.

BODY

Cast on 9 sts.

Work 2 rows in garter stitch.

Next row: Increase 1 st at each
end of row (11 sts).

Work 1 row.

Repeat the last 2 rows, four
times (19 sts).

Next row: K9, increase before
and after centre stitch, k9
(21 sts).

Continue to increase in this
manner (either side of centre
stitch) on every alt row until
there are 45 sts.

Work a further 31 rows
without shaping.

Next row: Decrease 1 st at each
end of this and every following
alt row until there are 21 sts.

Next row: (K2tog) five times,
k1, (k2tog) five times.

Cast off.

Make another piece to match.

ARMS

Cast on 7 sts.

Work 1 row.

Next row: K1 (inc 1, k1) to end
(13 sts).

Repeat the last 2 rows once
more (25 sts).

Work 1 row.

Next row: K6, inc 1, k1, inc 1,
k11, inc 1, k1, inc 1, k6 (29 sts).

Work a further 28 rows
without shaping.

SHAPE TOP OF ARMS

Decrease 1 st at each end of
this and every following 6th
row until there are 17 sts, then
on every following 3rd row
until there are 11 sts.

Next row: K1 (k2tog) to end
(6 sts).

Cast off.

Make another piece to match.

LEGS

Cast on 46 sts.

Work 12 rows.

Next row: Decrease 1 st at each
end of row (44 sts).

Cast off 2 sts at the beg of the
next 2 rows (40 sts).

Cast off 4 sts at the beg of the
next 2 rows (32 sts).

Work a further 31 rows
without shaping.

Cast off 4 sts at the beg of the
next 2 rows (24 sts).

Cast off 4 sts at the beg of the
next 2 rows (16 sts).

Cast off remaining stitches.

Make another leg to match.

PAW PADS

Cast on 5 sts. Work in garter
stitch.

Work 1 row.

Next row: Increase 1 st, at each
end of this and every following
alt row, until there are 13 sts.

Work a further 6 rows without
shaping.

Next row: Decrease 1 st, at
each end of every alt row, until
there are 8 sts.

Cast off.

Make another pad to match.

EARS – 2 PIECES EACH EAR

Beginning at the top of the
ear, cast on 16 sts.

Work in garter stitch.

Work 1 row.

Next row: Increase 1 st at each
end of the row (18 sts).

Work 1 row.

Repeat the last 2 rows until
there are 24 sts.

Work a further 2 rows without
shaping.

Next row: Decrease 1 st at each end of this and every following alt row, until there are 16 sts. Cast off.
Make four pieces in total.

TO MAKE UP THE BEAR
Darn in all loose ends. Join head seam and stuff firmly. Sew ear sections together and position on head as illustrated. Leaving neck open, join all body pieces and attach head. Join both leg seams, inserting pads at the base, and stuff firmly. Repeat with arms. Attach arms and legs to body, ensuring that Teddy will sit steadily! Embroider on the eyes and nose.

Pink sweater

MATERIALS
- **Rowan Yorkshire Tweed DK:**
  2 x pink 350 (A)
- **Rowan 4-Ply Soft:**
  1 x white 376 * (B)
- Needles: 4mm/ UK size 8
- 2 small buttons

* Yarn to be used doubled

BACK

Using main yarn, cast on 50 sts.
Work 8 rows in k2 p2 rib.
Continue in stocking stitch, and
work 40 rows.
Shoulder shaping:
Cast off 15 sts at the beginning
of the next 2 rows (20 sts).
Cast off remaining sts.

FRONT

Using main yarn, cast on 50 sts.
Work 8 rows in k2 p2 rib.
Continue in stocking stitch, and
work 4 rows.
Using Fair Isle technique and
contrast yarn where indicated,
work the next 11 rows from
the chart.
Continue in stocking stitch
until 34 rows have been
completed from top of rib.

■ A
□ B

Divide for neck.
K20, cast off central 10 sts, K to
end.
Using these 20 sts only, work
1 row.
Next row: Decrease 1 st at neck
edge on this and following two
alt rows (17 sts).
Work 3 rows in stocking stitch.
Cast off.
Rejoin yarn to remaining 20 sts
and work to match first side,
reversing shapings.

SLEEVES

Using main yarn, cast on 40 sts.
Work 6 rows in k2 p2 rib.
Continue in stocking stitch, and
work 20 rows.
Cast off.
Make another sleeve.

NECKBAND

Join right-hand shoulder using

mattress stitch. With right side
facing, pick up 54 sts evenly
around the neck.
Work 5 rows in k2 p2 rib.
Cast off in pattern.

SHOULDER

Catch left side shoulder
together at sleeve edge
(approx 2.5cm).
Pick up 32 sts evenly from neck
edge, down to sleeve edge and
back up to other side of
neckband, and knit.
Next row: P.
Next row (buttonhole row):
K23, yfwd k2tog, k3, yfwd
k2tog, k2.
Next row: P.
Cast off.

TO MAKE UP SWEATER

Darn in all ends and sew
buttons to shoulder. Fold

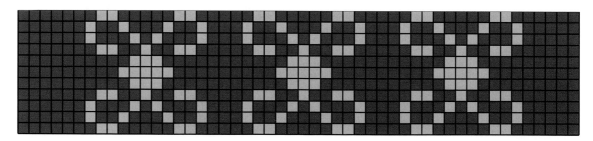

sleeves in half lengthways and, starting at the centre of the shoulder, sew on using mattress stitch. Join side and sleeve seams.

Blue sweater

MATERIALS
- **Rowan Yorkshire Tweed DK:**
  2 x light blue 347
- Needles: 4mm/ UK size 8
- Cable needle

BACK
Cast on 50 sts.
Work 8 rows in k2 p2 rib.
Continue in stocking stitch and work 42 rows.
Work 6 rows in k2 p2 rib.
Cast off.

FRONT
Cast on 50 sts.
Work 8 rows in k2 p2 rib.
Continue in stocking stitch and work 42 rows, inserting cable panel in centre of front panel – work 19 sts; set panel 13 sts; work 18 sts (50 sts).
Work 6 rows in k2 p2 rib.
Cast off.

SLEEVES
Work as for pink sweater.

TO MAKE UP SWEATER
Darn in all loose ends. Join front and back panels by a 2.5cm seam at shoulders, using mattress stitch to form slash neck. Attach sleeves.

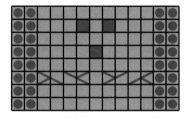

   Knit on RS, purl on WS

   Purl on RS, knit on WS

■   Make bobble (k1, p1, k1, p1, k1) in stitch to make 5 sts from one.
Turn, p5, turn, and pass 2nd, 3rd, 4th, 5th sts over first st one at a time, then knit into the back of it.

⬚   Sl next 2 sts on to cable needle and hold at front.

K2, then p2 from cable needle.

⬚   Sl next 2 sts on to cable needle and hold at back.
P2, then k2 from cable needle.

Ricky rabbit

This delightful, floppy-eared bunny likes to dress to impress his friends in the warren, loves meeting new people, and has got a great sense of humour. Who are you going to introduce him to?

MATERIALS

- **Rowan All Seasons Cotton:**
  2 x fawn 191
  2 x cream 178
- Black embroidery thread for eyes and mouth
- 50cm broad double satin ribbon
- Needles: 3.75mm/ UK size 9
- Toy stuffing

BODY – FRONT

Use cream. Cast on 20 sts and work 2 rows in stocking stitch. Increase 1 st at each end of next and following alternate row (24 sts).
Continue without further shaping until work measures 15cm from beginning.
Next row: Decrease 1 st at each end of next and every following 4th row until there are 12 sts.
Work 3 rows in stocking stitch. Cast off.

BODY – BACK

Use fawn.

Cast on 24 sts and work 2 rows in stocking stitch.
Increase 1 st at each end of this and following alternate row (28 sts).
Continue without further shaping until work measures 15cm from beginning.
Next row: Decrease 1 st at each end of next and every following 4th row until there are 16 sts.
Work 3 rows in stocking stitch. Cast off.

HEAD – BACK

Use fawn. Cast on 12 sts and work 2 rows in stocking stitch.
Next row: Increase 1 st at each end of row (14 sts).
Repeat this increase on every other row until there are 20 sts.
Work a further 8 rows in stocking stitch without shaping.
Next row: Decrease 1 st at each end of this and every following alternate row until there are

6 sts.
Cast off.

HEAD – FRONT

Use fawn.
Cast on 6 sts and work 2 rows in stocking stitch.
Next row: K1, increase 1 st, K to end of row (7 sts).
Next row: K1, P to last stitch, increase 1 st, k1 (8 sts).
Repeat the last 2 rows four times (16 sts).
Work a further 2 rows without shaping.
Next row: K2tog, K to end (15 sts).
Next row: P.
Repeat the last 2 rows four times (9 sts).
Continue to decrease on the same edge until 3 sts remain.
Next row: K1, p2tog. Cast off.
Work another piece the same, reversing all shaping.

EARS

Each made in two sections (one in fawn and one in cream).

following 4th row, until there are 11 sts.

Work a further 11 rows without shaping.

Next row: Decrease at each end of this and every following 8th row until 3 sts remain.

Next row: K1, p2tog, psso. Fasten off.

FEET
Use fawn.

Cast on 8 sts and work 2 rows in stocking stitch.

Next row: Increase 1 st at each end of row (10 sts).

Continue working in stocking stitch for a further 31 rows without shaping.

Cast off.

Make another foot to match.

ARMS
Use fawn.

Follow arm pattern for Mousie Mousie.

Make another arm to match.

TAIL
Use cream.

Make a pom-pom. Cut 2 circles of cardboard, approx 20cm in diameter, and cut out a circle in the centre of each to make a ring. Hold both rings together and start wrapping yarn around the ring, threading it through the centre, until completely covered. Position the point of a pair of scissors in the yarn loops so that you can cut through them, going in between the cardboard rings. Separate the rings slightly and tie yarn tightly inside the cut sections. Remove cardboard and fluff up the pom-pom. Sew to back of rabbit.

TO MAKE UP THE RABBIT
Join body pieces together using mattress stitch; stuff. Join side seams of both feet and arms, and pad slightly. Attach arms to shoulders of rabbit and sew on feet as illustrated. To form head, sew the shaped sides of the two front pieces together, then sew straight edge to back piece, leaving the cast-on edges open to stuff. Attach to body. Sew a cream and a fawn ear piece together. Repeat to make the other ear and attach to head. Embroider features. Tie ribbon around neck.

Using the appropriate yarn, cast on 5 sts and knit one row.

Next row: K1, P to last st, k1.

Continue working in stocking stitch, increasing 1 st at each end of next and every

Sleeveless top

MATERIALS
- **Rowan All Seasons Cotton:**
  1 x light blue 192
- Needles: 4.5mm/ UIK size 7

BACK
Cast on 22 sts.
Knit 2 rows.
Next row: Continue in stocking stitch until work measures 8cm ending with a WS row *.

SHAPE TOP OF BACK
K1, k2tog, work to last 3 sts, k2tog, k1 (20 sts).
Work 3 rows in stocking stitch.
Repeat the last 4 rows once more (18 sts).
Then work the decrease row once more (16 sts).
Next row: P.
Cast off.

FRONT
Work as for Back until you reach *.
Shape top and divide for neck:
k1, k2tog, k5, k2tog, k1.
Turn work and work on these 9 sts only.

Stocking stitch 3 rows.
Next row: K1, k2tog, k3, k2tog, k1 (7 sts).
Stocking stitch 3 rows.
Next row: K1, k2tog, k1, k2tog, k1 (5 sts).
Stocking stitch 3 rows.
Cast off.

Rejoin yarn to remaining sts, complete to match first side and cast off.

TO MAKE UP RABBIT'S TOP
Darn in all ends. Join shoulder seams using mattress stitch. Join side seams.

Penguin

Penguin is just the right size for little hands. She's ready to waddle into a new home and become a cherished companion. She has lots of stories to tell about her life in the Arctic, exploring snowy wastes and diving through the ice.

MATERIALS
- **Rowan Handknit Cotton:**
  1 x black 252
  1 x white 251
- Rowan Cotton Glace:
  1 x gold 802 *
- Black embroidery thread
- Needles: 4mm/ UK size 8
- Toy stuffing

*Yarn to be used doubled

BACK
Use black.
Cast on 20 sts and, working in stocking stitch, complete 26 rows.
Decrease 1 st at each end of next and every following 6th row until there are 10 sts.
Work 1 row *.
Decrease 1 st at each end of next and every following alt row until there are 6 sts.
Work 1 row.
Next row: K2tog, k2, k2tog (4 sts).
Next row: P.
Cast off.

FRONT
Use white.
Work as back until *.
Cast off.

BEAK TOP
Use gold.
Using yarn doubled, cast on 18 sts.
Work 4 rows in stocking stitch.
Decrease 1 st at each end of next 4 rows (10 sts).
Work 12 rows without further shaping.
Decrease 1 st at each end of next 3 rows (4 sts).
Next row: P.
Cast off.

BEAK BOTTOM
Use gold.
Using yarn doubled, cast on 5 sts.
Work 4 rows in stocking stitch.
Next row: K2tog, k1, k2tog (3 sts).
Starting with a purl row, work 13 rows in stocking stitch.
Next row: K1, k2tog (2 sts).

Purl.
Break yarn off, draw through loops and fasten off.

FEET
(Make two in black and two in gold.)
Using the appropriate yarn, cast on 7 sts.
Work 2 rows in stocking stitch.
Increase 1 st at each end of this and every following alternate row until there are 11 sts.
Work 5 rows in stocking stitch.
Decrease 1 st at each end of next and every following alternate row until there are 5 sts.
Purl.
Cast off.

LEFT FLIPPER
Use black.
Cast on 3 sts.
Work 1 row in purl.
Next row: * Increase 1 st at beginning of this and every following alternate row until

there are 10 sts.
Work 16 rows in stocking stitch.
Shape top of flipper:
Work to last 3 sts, k2tog, k1 (9 sts).
Next row: P.

Continue to decrease at the end of next and every following alternate row until there are 5 sts.
Work 1 row.
Cast off.

RIGHT FLIPPER
Work as Left Flipper to *.
Increase 1 st at end of this and every following alternate row until there are 10 sts.
Work 16 rows in stocking stitch.
Complete to match left side, reversing shaping at the top.

TO MAKE UP PENGUIN
Darn in all loose ends. Join main body panels using mattress stitch, leaving the top open. Stuff firmly. Join beak parts, stuffing them slightly. Attach beak to top of body as illustrated, and stitch the eyes in black embroidery thread. Using mattress stitch, join the black and gold feet pieces, padding them firmly. Close them completely and then attach to the main body, with the gold showing on top. Apply flippers to each side of the main body along side seam.

Kangaroo and baby roo

This cute and cuddly double act have travelled a long way from sunny Australia. Kangaroo has prepared for chilly breezes with a dashing scarf; baby roo just snuggles down in the pouch. They're just looking for someone to show them all the sights in their new home country.

MATERIALS

- **Rowan All Seasons Cotton:**
  4 x gold 205
  1 x cream 178
- **Rowan Yorkshire Tweed 4-ply:**
  1 x green 272
- Black embroidery thread for eyes
- Needles: 4mm/ UK size 8, 3.75mm/ UK size 9, 3mm/ UK size 11
- Toy stuffing

Use 4mm/ UK size 8 needles for the kangaroo.

BODY – SIDE
Use gold.
Cast on 34 sts.
Work 9 rows in stocking stitch.
Next row: Cast off 16 sts, P to end (18 sts).
Row 11: K to last st, inc at end of row (19 sts).
Row 12: Inc 1 st at beg of row, P to end (20 sts).

Row 13: K to last st, inc at end of row (21 sts).
Row 14: As row 12 (22 sts).
Row 15: K.
Row 16: As row 12 (23 sts).
Row 17: K.
Row 18: P (24 sts).
Work a further 15 rows in stocking stitch without shaping.
Row 34: P2tog, work to end (23 sts).
Row 35: K.
Row 36: Cast off 7 sts, P to end (16 sts).
Row 37: K to last st, inc at end of row (17 sts).
Row 38: P.
Row 39: As row 37 (18 sts).
Work a further 3 rows in stocking stitch without shaping.
Row 43: K2tog, K to end (17 sts).
Row 44: P.
Row 45: As row 43 (16 sts).
Row 46: P.

Row 47: As row 43 (15 sts).
Row 48: P.
Row 49: As row 43 (14 sts).
Work a further 8 rows in stocking stitch without shaping.
Row 58: Dec 1 st at beg of row, work to end (13 sts).
Row 59: Dec 1 st at beg of row, work to end (12 sts).
Work a further 6 rows in stocking stitch without shaping.
Row 66: Cast on 7 sts, work to end (19 sts).
Row 67: K.
Row 68: P2tog, work to end (18 sts).
Row 69: K.
Row 70: As row 68 (17 sts).
Row 71: K.
Row 72: As row 68 (16 sts).
Row 73: K2tog, work to end.
Row 74: As row 68 (15 sts).
Row 75: K2tog, work to end (14 sts).
Row 76: K2tog, work to last

2 sts, k2tog (12 sts).
Row 77: K2tog at each end of row (10 sts).
Cast off.
Make another piece, reversing all shaping.

BODY – FRONT
Use cream.
Cast on 40 sts.
Work 9 rows in stocking stitch.
Row 10: Cast off 16 sts, work to end (24 sts).
Row 11: Cast off 16 sts, work to end (8 sts).
Row 12: Increase 1 st at each end of row (10 sts).
Row 13: Increase 1 st at each end of row (12 sts).
Row 14: Increase 1 st at each end of row (14 sts).
Row 15: K.
Row 16: Increase 1 st at each end of row (16 sts).
Row 17: K.
Row 18: Increase 1 st at each end of row (18 sts).
Row 19: K.
Row 20: Increase 1 st at each end of row (20 sts).
Work a further 17 rows without shaping.
Row 38: Cast off 6 sts at beg of

row, work to end (14 sts).
Row 39: Cast off 6 sts at beg of row, work to end (8 sts).
Work on these 8 sts until work measures the same as the body sides to beg of head shaping.
Cast off.

BODY – BASE
Use gold.
Cast on 10 sts.
Work 18 rows in stocking stitch.
Cast off.

EARS
Use gold 205.
Cast on 7 sts.
Work 8 rows in garter stitch (every row knit).
Next row: K2tog, k3, k2tog (5 sts).
Next row: K.
Next row: K2tog, k1, k2tog (3 sts).
Next row: K.
Next row: K2tog, k1 (2 sts).
Next row: K2tog (1 st).
Fasten off.
Make another ear to match.

ARMS
Use gold.

Follow arm instructions for Mousie Mousie on pages 70–71.
Make two arms.

TAIL
Use gold.
Follow tail instructions for Mousie Mousie on pages 70–71 and work 28 rows without shaping.

POUCH
Cast on 14 sts.
Moss stitch 1 row.
Next row: Continue in moss stitch and Increase 1 st at each end of row (16 sts).
Work 2 rows without shaping.
Continue to increase 1 st at each end of next and every following 3rd row until there are 22 sts.
Next row: Work in k1 p1 rib to end.
Work 2 rows in rib without further shaping.
Cast off in pattern.

SCARF
Use green.
Using 3mm needles, cast on 7 sts and garter stitch (every

row knit) for approx 20cm.
Cast off.

TO MAKE UP KANGAROO
Darn in all loose ends. Sew two body sides together using mattress stitch, and attach to front panel. Stuff firmly, ensuring the base is squarely placed at the bottom. Attach pouch to body using mattress stitch. Join arm and tail seams and stuff. Sew arms to main body at shoulder, and position tail at base. Embroider eyes. Tie scarf loosely around neck.

BABY ROO
Use gold and 3.75mm/ UK size 9 needles.

BODY – SIDE PANEL
Starting at feet, cast on 10 sts.
Work 4 rows in stocking stitch.
5th row: Cast off 5 sts, K to end (5 sts).
Work a further 7 rows without shaping.
13th row: Cast on 4 sts, K to end (9 sts).
Work a further 3 rows without shaping.
17th row: Cast off 4 sts, K to end (5 sts).
Work a futher 2 rows without shaping.
20th row: P2tog, p3 (4 sts).
21st row: K.
22nd row: P2tog, p2 (3 sts).
23rd row: Cast on 4 sts, K to end (7 sts).
24th row: P2tog, P to end (6 sts).
25th row: K2tog, K to end (5 sts).
26th row: P.
27th row: K2tog, k3.
Cast off.
Work second side to match this, reversing all shaping.

BODY – FRONT PANEL
Cast on 14 sts.
Work 4 rows in stocking stitch.
5th row: Cast off 5 sts, K to end (9 sts).
6th row: Cast off 5 sts, P to end (4 sts).
Work a further 8 rows without shaping.
15th row: Cast on 4 sts, K to end (8 sts).
16th row: Cast on 4 sts, P to end (12 sts).
Work a further 3 rows without shaping.
20th row: Cast off 4 sts, P to end (8 sts).
21st row: Cast off 4 sts, K to end (4 sts).
22nd row: P2tog twice.
23rd row: K2tog, fasten off.

EARS
Cast on 2 sts.
Work 4 rows in garter stitch.
Next row: K2tog twice.
Next row: K2.
Next row: K2tog, fasten off.
Make another ear to match.

TAIL
Cast on 4 sts.
Work 16 rows in garter stitch.
Next row: K2tog twice.
Next row: K2.
Next row: K2tog, fasten off.

TO MAKE UP BABY ROO
Darn in all loose ends. Sew the two sides together along back seam and leave a small opening for stuffing. Sew in front panel, starting at bottom feet. Stuff firmly and close seam in the back. Sew in ears, folding them slightly at the base. Attach tail. Embroider the eyes.

Loulou the elephant

Share all your secrets with Loulou, a gentle woolly giant, who will never forget them. This sturdy creature is a delight to knit.

MATERIALS
- **Rowan Yorkshire Tweed DK**: 4 x grey 354
- **Rowan Cotton Glace**: Oddments of white 726
- Needles: 4mm/ UK size 8, 3mm/ UK size 11
- Toy stuffing

Use 4mm/ UK size 8 needles and grey yarn for all parts of elephant except for tusks.

HEAD – SIDE SECTIONS
Cast on 25 sts.
Knit 1 row.
Continue in stocking stitch throughout. Increase 1 st at each end of the next 2 rows (29 sts).
Work a further 11 rows without shaping.
Next row: Increase 1 st at each end of row (31 sts).
Work a further 12 rows without shaping.
Next row: K2tog at each end of row (29 sts).
Work a further 14 rows without shaping.
Next row: K2tog at each end

of the following 5 rows (19 sts).
Cast off.
Make another piece to match.

HEAD – CENTRE GUSSET, TOP
Cast on 9 sts.
Work 7 rows in stocking stitch.
Next row: Increase 1 st at each end of row (9 sts).
Repeat the last 8 rows seven times (23 sts).
Work a further 30 rows without shaping.
Next row: Decrease 1 st at each end of row (21 sts).
Work a further 11 rows without shaping.
Repeat the last 1 row eight times (5 sts).
Cast off.

HEAD – CENTRE GUSSET, UNDER TRUNK
Cast on 7 sts.
Work 11 rows in stocking stitch.
Next row: Increase 1 st at each end of row.
Repeat the last 12 rows five times.
Cast off.

EARS
Ears are worked in garter stitch throughout.
Cast on 17 sts.
Knit 1 row.
Next row: Increase 1 st at each end of the following 6 rows (29 sts).
Next row: K to last stitch, increase twice (31 sts).
Work a further 18 rows without shaping.
Next row: (K2tog, k3) to last st, k1 (25 sts).
Next row: K2tog three times, k5, k2tog three times.
Cast off remaining stitches.
Make another ear to match.

BODY – FRONT AND BACK
Cast on 20 sts.
Work in stocking stitch throughout.
Work 2 rows.
Next row: Increase 1 st at each end of this and every following alternate row until there are 30 sts.
Next row: Increase 1 st at each end of this and every following 4th row until there are 40 sts.

Work a further 24 rows without shaping.
Next row: Decrease 1 st at each end of this and every following 4th row until there are 20 sts.
Next row: K2tog, K to end.
Cast off.

ARMS
Cast on 25 sts.
Work 22 rows in stocking stitch.
Cast off.
Make another arm to match.

LEGS
Cast on 30 sts.
Work 30 rows in stocking stitch.
Cast off.
Make another leg to match.

PADS – FOR ARMS
Cast on 6 sts.
Work 2 rows in stocking stitch.
Next row: Increase 1 st at each end of row (8 sts).
Next row: P.
Next row: Increase 1 st at each end of row (10 sts).
Work a further 5 rows without shaping.
Next row: Decrease 1 st at each end of following 2 alt rows (6 sts).
Cast off.
Make another pad to match.

PADS – FOR LEGS
Cast on 6 sts.
Work 2 rows in stocking stitch.
Next row: Increase 1 st at each end of this and following 2 alternate rows (12 sts).
Work a further 5 rows without shaping.
Next row: Decrease 1 st at each end of this and following 2 alt rows (6 sts).
Cast off.
Make another pad to match.

TAIL
Cast on 7 sts.
Work 14 rows in stocking stitch.
Next row: Decrease 1 st at each end of this and every following 4th row until there are 3 sts.
Work a further 3 rows without shaping.
Break yarn and draw through remaining stitches. Fasten off.
Cut short lengths of yarn, knot together, place in the point of the tail, and sew side seam using mattress stitch.

TUSKS
Use the 3mm/ UK size 11 needles and white yarn.
Cast on 7 sts.
Work in stocking stitch for 30 rows.
Next row: K1, k2tog, k1, k2tog, k1 (5 sts).
Next row: P.
Next row: K2tog, k1, k2tog (3 sts).
Next row: P.
Next row: K3tog and fasten off.
Make another tusk to match.

TO MAKE UP THE ELEPHANT
Darn in all loose ends. Join all pieces using mattress stitch. Attach sides of head to main gusset. Insert lower gusset and stuff, leaving neck edges open. Join body sections and sew on head. Sew side seams of arms and legs and insert pads; stuff. Attach to body (make sure elephant will sit on a flat surface). Sew on tail. Join tusk seams and draw up to make the tusk curve slightly. Sew on under the trunk. Add features.

Mousie Mousie

Childhood memories have been recaptured in this cheeky little mouse – my brothers kept mice and always had lots of fun with them! Mousie Mousie is a personable character who sports a woolly scarf to keep him snug. He's got a friendly face, a slithery tail and would be good company for any child.

MATERIALS
- **Rowan Handknit Cotton:**
  1 x fawn 205
  1 x cream 251
- **Rowan Yorkshire Tweed 4-ply:**
  1 x green 272
- Oddments of black embroidery thread for eyes
- Needles: 4mm/ UK size 8
- Double-pointed needles: 2 x 4mm/ UK size 11

HEAD
Use fawn.
Make two pieces. Please note that one piece must be knitted in reverse stocking stitch.
Cast on 17 sts.
Stocking stitch 2 rows.
Inc 1 st at each end of next and every following alt row until there are 27 sts.
Work 4 rows without shaping.
Next row: K1, (k2tog) twice, K to last 3 sts, k2tog, k1 (24 sts).
Next row: P.

Repeat the last two rows once more (21 sts).
Decrease 1 st at each end of next and every following alt row until there are 13 sts.
Next row: P.
Cast off 4 sts at the beginning of next 2 rows (5 sts).
Cast off remaining 5 sts.

EARS
Use fawn.
Cast on 7 sts. Knit in garter stitch.
Knit 2 rows.
Increase in first and last stitch of next row (9 sts).
Next row: K.
Increase in first and last stitch of next row (11 sts).
Next row: K.
Work 3 increase rows as before (17 sts).
Garter stitch 3 rows.
K2tog at each end of every row until there are 9 sts.
Garter stitch 1 row.

Cast off.
Make another ear to match.

BODY – FRONT
Use cream.
Cast on 5 sts. Knit in stocking stitch.
Increase either side of centre stitch (7 sts).
Work 1 row.
Increase at the beginning and end of row, and as before on either side of centre st (11 sts).
Work 1 row.
Repeat the last 2 rows until there are 39 sts.
Work 2 rows without shaping.
Decrease 1 st at each end of work on next and every alt row until there are 29 sts.
Decrease on either side of centre stitch only, on next and every alt row until 17 sts remain.
Work 1 row.
Cast off.

BODY – BACK

Use fawn.

Cast on 5 sts.

1st row: Increase in every st.

2nd row: P.

3rd row: Increase 1 st at each end of next and every alt row until there are 22 sts.

Stocking stitch 4 rows.

Dec 1 st at each end of row (20 sts).

Work 1 row.

Repeat last 2 rows until there are 14 sts.

Continue without shaping until work matches front body section.

Cast off.

ARMS

Use fawn.

Cast on 6 sts.

Stocking stitch 2 rows.

Increase 1 st at each end of next and following alt rows until there are 14 sts.

Work 1 row.

Stocking stitch 16 rows.

K1 (k2tog) six times, k1 (8 sts).

Work 1 row without shaping.

K2tog to end (4 sts).

Break thread and draw through remaining sts and secure.

Make another arm to match.

FEET

Use fawn.

Cast on 8 sts.

Stocking stitch 2 rows.

Increase in first and last st of next row (10 sts).

Stocking stitch 18 rows.

Cast off.

Make another foot to match.

SCARF

Use light green.

Cast on 10 sts.

Garter stitch to length required: approx 30cm.

Cast off.

TAIL

Use cream.

Using two double-pointed needles, cast on 7 sts.

Knit to end. Instead of turning work, slide from one end of the needle to the other, keeping right side facing at all times, and continue to knit. This forms a tube.

Knit to desired length.

Cast off.

TO MAKE UP MOUSIE MOUSIE

Join head pieces using mattress stitch and stuff. Join front and back body pieces in the same manner and secure to head. Sew on ears and tail. Join arm seams and stuff arms slightly; sew into position. Join seams of feet and sew pieces into a round. Sew to body, ensuring that they are in a position for the mouse to stand. Darn in the ends of the scarf and wrap around. Sew eyes and nose, using black embroidery thread as illustrated.

Reggie the snake

Have fun with this easy-to-knit snake. He will bring a smile to the face of any little boy.

MATERIALS
- **Rowan Summer Tweed:**
  2 x green 527
- **Rowan Yorkshire Tweed 4-ply:**
  1 x red 274 *
- Oddments of yarn or embroidery thread for eyes and detail on back
- Needles: 4mm/ UK size 8
- Toy stuffing

*Yarn to be used doubled

MAIN BODY
Use green.

Cast on 7 sts and, working in stocking stitch, complete 2 rows.

Row 3: Increase 1 st at each end of work (9 sts).

Row 4: P.

Row 5: K.

Row 6: P.

Row 7: Increase 1 st at each end of work (11 sts).

Repeat the last 4 rows once more until there are 13 sts.

Continue in stocking stitch for a further 13 rows without shaping.

Next row: Increase 1 st at each end of row (15 sts).

Work a further 13 rows without shaping.

Increase on next and every 14th row until there are 29 sts.

Work without further shaping until snake measures 104cm from cast-on, ending on a purl row.

SHAPE HEAD
With RS facing, k14, cast off 1 st and K to end.

Working on the first 14 sts only, P.

Next row: K2tog, work to last 2 sts, k2tog (12 sts).

Work 3 rows without shaping.

Repeat the last 4 rows until 4 sts remain.

Cast off.

Rejoin yarn to remaining 14 sts and complete to match first side.

MOUTH LINING
Use red.

Using yarn doubled, cast on 4 sts and stocking stitch 2 rows.

Next row: Increase 1 st at each end of the row (6 sts).

Work 3 rows in stocking stitch.

Next row: Increase 1 st at each end of the row (8 sts).

Repeat the last 4 rows until there are 28 sts.

Work a further 12 rows without shaping.

With RS facing, decrease 1 st at each end of row.

Work 3 rows in stocking stitch.

Repeat the last 4 rows until 4 sts remain.

Cast off.

TO MAKE UP SNAKE
Darn in all loose ends. Join side seams using mattress stitch and stuff firmly. Insert mouth piece and slightly pad head. Darn eyes and embroider detail on the back of the snake as illustrated.

Nursery toys
and accessories

Each of these projects is designed for a baby or young child. From the starfish to the glove puppets they're all delightfully easy to knit and can all be given a character of their own by trying out different colours and facial expressions. The nursery balls and blocks are classic toys that any new parent would be delighted to have for their new baby. The two knitted bags are the end could be used to store your toys in or given to a little girl to carry around with her.

Starfish

Living by the beach, I always hoped to find a beautiful starfish just like this one amongst the pebbles. Keep him to remind you of sunny days by the sea. He's ideal for a baby or young child to cuddle, and would even make a great doorstop!

MATERIALS
- **Rowan All Seasons Cotton:**
  1 x cream 178
  1 x light blue 192
  1 x sea blue 185
- Needles: 4.5mm/ UK size 7
- Toy stuffing

Knit ten panels: five are cream; five are a mixture of blues.

PANEL
Cast on 3 sts and stocking stitch 2 rows.
Next row: Increase 1 st at each end of next and every following 6th row until there are 19 sts.
Next row: P.

SHAPE TOP OF PANEL
K1, k2tog, K to last 3 sts, k2tog, k1 (17 sts).
Next row: P.
Repeat the last two rows until 5 sts remain.
K1, k2tog, pass stitch back from the right-hand needle to the left-hand needle, k2tog, k1 (3 sts).
Break yarn and draw through.

TO MAKE UP THE STARFISH
Darn in all ends.
Join all sections, leaving adequate seams to allow for stuffing. Close all seams using mattress stitch.

Nursery ball

These delightful knitted toys will be a welcome addition to any nursery. They are made in a combination of hearts and stripes.

MATERIALS
(Ball with hearts)
- **Rowan Cotton Glace:**
  1 x white 726 (A)
  1 x sea green 809 (B)

(Ball with stripes)
- **Rowan Cotton Glace:**
  1 x white 726
  1 x muted pink 747
  1 x sky blue 749
- Needles: 3mm/ UK size 11
- Toy stuffing

Each nursery ball uses approximately 50 grams of yarn

Each ball is made up of 6 panels.

PANEL
Cast on 1 st, k1.
Next row: Purl into front, back and front (3 sts).
Continue in stocking stitch, increasing 1 st at each end of next and following 2 alternate rows (9 sts).
Work 2 rows without shaping.
Increase 1 st at each end of

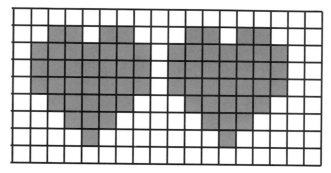

☐ **A**

▦ **B**

next and following 3rd row, then at each end of following 4th row (15 sts).
Work 5 rows without further shaping.
Increase at each end of next and following 6th row. (19 sts).
Work 9 rows without further shaping.
(Set heart motif within these 9 straight rows if required – follow chart.)
Decrease once at each end of next and every following 6th row until there are 13 sts.
Decrease at each end of following 4th row, following 3rd row and next alternate row (7 sts).

Work 1 row, then decrease 1 st at each end of the next 2 rows (3 sts).
Next row: Sl1, k2tog, psso. Fasten off.

For striped version, work as above, changing colour every two rows.

TO MAKE UP THE BALL

Darn in all loose ends. Mattress stitch pieces together alternating the striped and plain, or motif and plain sections. Leave one seam open for inserting stuffing. Stuff, then close last seam.

Nursery blocks

Keep your toddlers happy with these pretty nursery blocks. They are knitted with motifs, interesting textures, and a variety of colours.

MATERIALS
(Block with hearts)
- **Rowan Cotton Glace:**
    1 x sky blue 749 (A)
    1 x white 726 (B)
    1 x lilac 811
    1 x muted green 814 (C)
(Blocks with anchors)
- **Rowan Cotton Glace:**
    1 x white 726
    1 x light brown 730
    1 x sky blue 749

- Needles: 3mm/ UK size 11
- Toy stuffing
- Bell(s) (optional)

Each nursery block uses approximately 50 grams of yarn. Each block is made up of 6 squares.

PLAIN OR HEART SQUARE
Cast on 27 sts and moss stitch 3 rows.

Next row: Keeping a border of 3 moss sts on either side, stocking stitch 30 rows (insert heart motif in centre if required – follow chart: work 4 sts, set motif 19 sts, work 4 sts).
Moss stitch 3 rows.
Cast off.

□ A   ■ B   ■ C

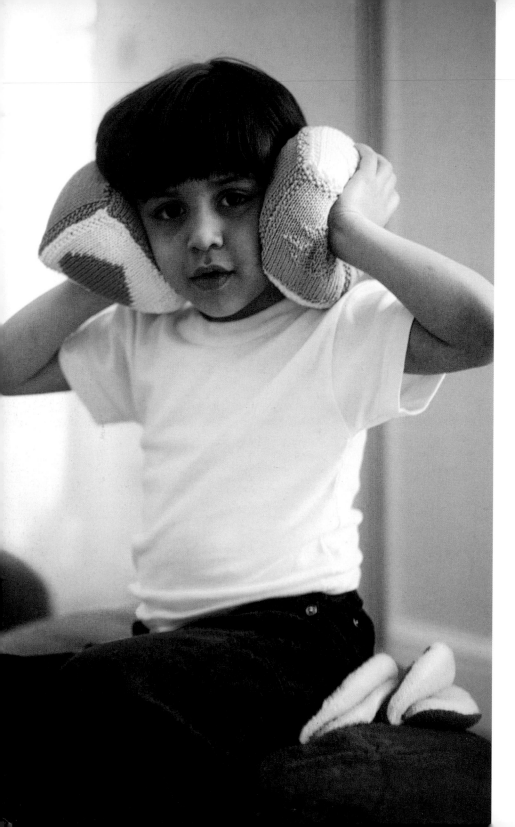

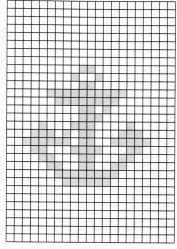

☐ **K on RS, P on WS**
☐ **P on RS, K on WS**

TO MAKE UP NURSERY
BLOCK
Darn in all ends. Join all
squares using mattress stitch,
leaving small opening for
stuffing.
Insert bell if required, at this
stage. Stuff. Close seam.

Finger puppets

Children can create their own production with these finger puppets! They will ensure imaginative play and give hours of pleasure. Once you've mastered the simple pattern for the basic body, and have tried the octopus and mouse, delight and amuse your children by devising your own creatures to add to the cast.

MATERIALS
- **Rowan Cotton Glace:** oddments
- Needles: 3mm/ UK size 11
- Toy stuffing

BASIC BODY
Cast on 15 sts.
Knit 2 rows.
Continue in stocking stitch, beginning with a knit row, until work measures 6cm from cast-on; end on a purl row *.
Next row: Shape top. (K1, k2tog), repeat to end (10 sts).
Next row: P.
Next row: (K2tog) to end (5 sts).
Break yarn and draw through remaining stitches. Fasten off and join seam.

Octopus

BODY
Use blue yarn. Follow instructions for basic body to *.
Next row (make head): Increase. K1, * make 1, k1, repeat from * to end of row (29 sts).
Work 11 rows in moss stitch.
Next row: Decrease. K1, * k2tog, repeat from * to end (15 sts).
Next row: P.
Next row: K1, * k2tog, repeat from * to end (8 sts).
Break yarn and draw through remaining stitches. Fasten off.

LEGS
Using a contrasting shade of blue, cast on 5 sts.
Continue in stocking stitch until work measures 7cm.
Cast off.
Make a total of 8 legs.

TO MAKE UP THE OCTOPUS

Darn in all loose ends.
Join main seam on head and body piece, stuff head section. With running stitch, sew around bottom of head and draw up and secure (enclosing stuffing). Attach legs evenly around the body at the bottom of the head. Embroider smiley face as illustrated.

Mouse

BODY

Using cream yarn, follow instructions for basic body.

TAIL

Using cream yarn, cast on 5 sts. Work in stocking stitch for 11cm.
Next row: K2tog, k1, k2tog (3 sts).
Next row: P.
Next row: K3tog.
Cast off.
Pull work slightly – this allows it to coil into a roll.

EARS

Using cream yarn, cast on 4 sts. Work 2 rows in stocking stitch.
Next row: Continue in stocking stitch, increasing 1 st at each end of this and every alt row, until there are 14 sts.
Work a further 3 rows without shaping.
Next row: Decrease 1 st at each end of this and every following row until there are 2 sts.
Next row: K2tog, fasten off.
Make another ear to match.

TO MAKE UP MOUSE

Darn in all loose ends. Attach tail and ears. Embroider face and whiskers as illustrated.

Cat nightdress case

Tuck your nightdress safely away and this smiley cat will keep it warm. She likes to laze on the bed all day and be close at hand for last-minute cuddles before bedtime.

MATERIALS
- **Rowan All Seasons Cotton:** 2 x gold 205
- Black embroidery thread for eyes and mouth
- Needles: 4.5mm/ UK size 7
- Remnant of fabric: 70cm x 60cm
- Lining (optional): 70cm x 60cm
- Ribbon to decorate: 1m
- Toy stuffing

HEAD – SIDES
Cast on 17 sts and work 6 rows in garter stitch (every row knit).
Next row: Increase 1 st at beg of row, K to end (18 sts).
Next row: K to last stitch, increase in last st (19 sts).
Next row: Cast on 7 sts, K to end (26 sts).
Work 5 rows without shaping.
Next row: K to last st, increase in last st (27 sts).
Work 7 rows without shaping.
Next row: K2tog, K to end (26 sts).
Next row: K to last 2 sts, k2tog (25 sts).
Repeat the last 2 rows six times (19 sts).
Work 1 row.
Next row: K to last 2 sts, k2tog (18 sts).
Next row: K2tog, K to last 2 sts, k2tog (16 sts).
Work 1 row.
Repeat the last 2 rows twice (12 sts).
Cast off.
Work another piece to match.

HEAD – GUSSET
Starting at nose, cast on 2 sts.
Knit 1 row.
Next row: Increase 1 st at each end of row (4 sts).
Repeat the last 2 rows four times (12 sts).
Work 2 rows.
Next row: Increase 1 st at each end of row (14 sts).
Repeat the last 3 rows four times (22 sts).
Work 16 rows without shaping.
Next row: K2tog, K to last 2 sts, k2tog (20 sts).
Work 3 rows.
Next row: K2tog, K to last 2 sts, k2tog (18 sts).
Repeat the last 4 rows six times (6 sts).
Cast off.

EARS
Cast on 3 sts.
Work 2 rows.
Next row: Increase 1 st at each end of row (5 sts).
Repeat the last 3 rows until there are 17 sts.
Work 2 rows without further shaping.
Cast off.
Make another 3 pieces.

TO MAKE UP NIGHTDRESS CASE
Sew the gusset between the two sides of the head, starting at the nose. Join the two side sections under the nose to the chin, leaving neck open. Stuff firmly. Close neck by sewing with running stitch and gathering the work; secure tightly. Embroider eyes, nose, mouth and whisker features as

illustrated. Sew each pair of ear pieces together, then attach to head, gathering the wide edge slightly.

BAG

Lay out fabric, wrong side up, and fold a hem along each 70cm edge. Sew in place. With right sides together, put the newly hemmed edges together and sew, leaving an opening of approx 20–25cm in the middle of the seam. Sew the bottom of the bag together, ensuring the open seam is in the middle of the bag (not on the side). Insert a lining at this stage if required, using the same method, securing it in each of the two bottom corners, and sewing together at the opening. Make a hem on the top of the bag and sew. Gather the whole top of the bag using running stitch, ensuring that the cat's head fits neatly into it. Tack the head in place, with the opening at the back and sew. Add ribbon to decorate.

Frilly Top Bag

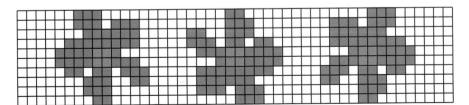

MATERIALS

- **Rowan Cotton Glace:**
  - 1 x white 726 (A)
  - 1 x 811 (B)
  - 1 x muted green 814 (C)
  - 1 x 815 (D)
- Needles: 3.25mm/ UK size 10
- 3.25mm double pointed needles

BACK

Cast on 46 stitches using yarn B and work two rows in stocking stitch.

Change to yarn A work a further two rows in stocking stitch.

Continue working in this striped sequence for 18cm

Leave stitches on a stitch holder.

FRONT

Cast on 46 stitches using yarn A and work four rows in stocking stitch.

Following chart, complete the next ten rows using both fair isle and intarsia techniques.

With RS facing and starting with a knit row, continue in stocking stitch until wor measures 18cm

Leave stitches on a stitch holder.

FRILLY TOP

With RS of panels facing, join one side seam using mattress stitch and slide all stitches onto one needle.

Using yarn D knit one row.

Next row WS Inc in every stitch. (184)sts

Next row RS starting with a knit row work a further four rows in stocking stitch forming frilly edge.

Cast off.

MAKING UP

Darn in all loose ends of motifs. Join side seam using mattress stitch.

HANDLES

Make two

Using double pointed needles and yarn C cast on 5 sts.

Knit one row*

Without turning the work, slide the stitches across the left needle (from left to right) up to the point.

Bring the yarn across the back of the work from left to right and pull tightly. Knit the next row as before and repeat from *

Continue until work measures 26cm.

Darn in loose ends and sew securely onto both sides of the bag at the base of the frill.

 A

 B

C

Knitted bag

Knitted in brightly coloured stripes and hearts, this little bag could be very useful for outings with Mum! The design uses only the most basic of knitting stitches, so it is an ideal project for beginners.

MATERIALS
- **Rowan Cotton Glace:**
  1 x muted green 814 (A)
  1 x dark pink 724 (B)
  1 x muted pink 747 (C)
  1 x white 726 (D)
- Needles: 3.25mm/ UK size 10
- Crochet hook: 3mm

TENSION
23 stitches, 32 rows
to 2.5cm (1in).
Finished bag is 10cm (4in)
square.

MAIN BODY OF BAG
Cast on 46 sts.
Knit in stocking stitch
throughout.
Follow Chart A for front and
Chart B for back, setting motifs
where desired.

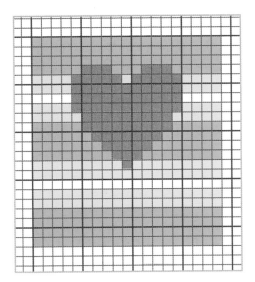

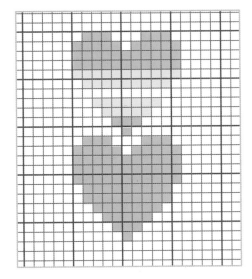

	A
	B
	C
	D

CHART A
Knitted in stripe sequence with green heart motif in intarsia.

CHART B
White background with two intarsia heart motifs.

When length of 18cm has been knitted, knit one row of holes as follows:
K1, * yfwd, k2tog. Rep from * to end.
Continue in stocking stitch for 2cm.
Cast off.
To form picot edge, fold work at row of holes and slipstitch in place.

HANDLES
Cast on 12 sts.
Stocking stitch to length required.
Cast off.

TO MAKE UP BAG
Sew two bag pieces along sides and bottom, with picot edge at top. Sew handles to inside of the bag.

Tension information

Rowan Cotton Glace
23 sts and 32 rows to 10cm
measured over stocking stitch
on 3mm/ UK size 11 needles.

Rowan All Seasons Cotton
18 sts and 25 rows to 10cm
measured over stocking stitch
on 4.5mm/ UK size 7 needles.

Rowan Handknit Cotton
20 sts and 28 rows to 10cm
measured over stocking stitch
on 4mm/ UK size 8 needles.

Rowan Yorkshire Tweed DK
22 sts and 30 rows to 10cm
measured over stocking stitch
on 4mm/ UK size 8 needles.

Rowan Yorkshire Tweed 4-ply
28 sts and 40 rows to 10cm
measured over stocking stitch
on 3mm/ UK size 11 needles.

Rowan 4-ply Soft – used double
22 sts and 30 rows to 10cm
measured over stocking stitch
on 4mm/ UK size 8 needles.

Please note: If used single, tension of this yarn would normally be:
28 sts and 36 rows to 10cm measured over stocking stitch on 3.25mm/ UK size 10 needles.

Rowan Summer Tweed
16 sts and 23 rows to 10cm
measured over stocking stitch
on 5mm/ UK size 8 needles.

Yarn information

Rowan Yorkshire Tweed 4-ply
100% wool.

Rowan Yorkshire Tweed DK
100% wool.

Rowan Cotton Glace
Lightweight, 100% cotton yarn, approximately 115m (125yds) per 50g (1¾oz) ball.

Rowan Handknit Cotton
Medium-weight 100% cotton yarn, approximately 85m (92yds) per 50g (1¾oz) ball.

Rowan Summer Tweed
100% wool.

Rowan 4-ply Soft
100% merino wool, approximately 175m (191yds) per 50g (1¾oz) ball.

Rowan All Seasons Cotton
60% cotton and 40% acrylic/ microfibre, approximately 90m (98yds) per 50g (1¾oz) ball.

Useful addresses & suppliers

Suppliers of Rowan Yarns

Australia
Rowan at Sunspun
185 Canterbury Road
Canterbury
Victoria 3126
Tel: 03 9830 1609

Canada
Diamond Yarn
9697 St Laurent
Montreal
Quebec H3L 2N1
Tel: 514 388 6188

UK
John Lewis
Stores nationally including
Oxford Street
London
W1a 1EX
Tel: 020 7629 7711
www.johnlewis.com

Rowan Yarns
Green Mill Lane
Holmfirth
West Yorkshire
HD9 2DX
Tel: 01484 681881
www.knitrowan.com

USA
Westminster Fibers, Inc.
3 Northern Boulevard, Suite 3
Amherst
New Hampshire 03031
Tel: 603 886 5041

See the Rowan website
www.knitrowan.com for further
stockists around the world.

Knitting abbreviations

k	knit	alt	alternate	tbl	through back of loop		
p	purl	cont	continue				
st(s)	stitch(es)	patt	pattern	M1	make one stitch by picking up horizontal loop before next stitch and knitting into back of it		
inc	increas(e)(ing)	tog	together				
dec	decreas (e) (ing)	mm	millimeters				
st st	stockinette stitch (1 row k, 1 row p)	cm	centimeters				
		in	inch(es)				
garter st	garter stitch (k every row)	RS	right side				
		WS	wrong side	yfwd	yarn forward		
beg	begin(ning)	Sl 1	slip one stitch	yrn	yarn around needle		
foll	following	psso	pass slipped stitch over				
rem	remain(ing)			yon	yarn over needle		
rev	revers(e) (ing)	p2sso	pass 2 slipped stitches over	cn	cable needle		
rep	repeat						

Needle sizes and conversions

Knitting needles are sized according to a standard sizing system, whatever material they are made from. There are three different systems: a metric system used in Europe and the UK; a US system; and an old UK and Canadian system.

Converting weights and lengths

oz = g x 0.0352
g   = oz x 28.35
in = cm x 0.3937
cm = in x 2.54
yds = m x 0.9144
m   = yds x 1.0936

Old UK & Metric size	US size	Canadian size
10	15	000
9	13	00
8	11	0
7½	10½	1
7	10½	2
6½	10½	3
6	10	4
5½	9	5
5	8	6
4½	7	7
4	6	8
3¼	5	9
3¼	4	10
3	2/3	11
2¾	2	12
2¼	1	13
2	0	14

Acknowledgements

Thank you to Mum for your endless support and countless hours of patient knitting and for teaching me the craft so many years ago, I will always be grateful. Thank you to Dad for my wonderful suppers and for the continual supply of tea. A huge Thank you must go to all of my family and friends who encouraged me throughout this project and kept me going, I couldn't of done it without you all!

I would like to Thank Kate Buller at Rowan Yarns for supporting me over the years and Thank you also to Rowan for supplying the beautiful yarns.

Thank you to Collins & Brown for the opportunity to make this book possible and in particular to Marie Clayton for your enthusiasm.

To all the ladies that have spent time with me and who have supported me at my workshops over the years, I thank you too!

My final words of gratitude must go to my partner Chris who has undeniably been a tower of strength throughout this long process. We can now go down the beach!